The Films of

ELIZABETH
TAYLOR

Heroes of the Movies – Elizabeth Taylor

Library of Congress Cataloging in Publication Data

d'Arcy, Susan.
The films of Elizabeth Taylor.

1. Taylor, Elizabeth, 1932-
I. Title.
PN2287.T18D3   1982   791.43′028′0924   [B]   82-12887
ISBN 0-8253-0110-6 (Beaufort Books)

Published in the United States by Beaufort Books, Inc.,
New York, and The Confucian Press, Inc.
Publishing simultaneously in Canada by
General Publishing Co. Limited

Printed in the U.S.A.   First Edition
10 9 8 7 6 5 4 3 2 1

The Films of
ELIZABETH
TAYLOR

Susan d'Arcy

THE CONFUCIAN PRESS, INC.

•

BEAUFORT BOOKS, INC.
New York/Toronto

4   Elizabeth Taylor, a legendary beauty and a consummate screen actress (to quote Richard Burton, who should know) was not a particularly beautiful baby. In fact she was a fairly average child — her eyes did not open for ten days and her back, head, ears and arms were covered in black fuzz. Her older brother, Howard, was an angelic little blond and family friends said what a pity it was that the looks in the family had gone to the boy. Nature soon redressed the balance. Her funny little nose suddenly developed a lovely shape. Her eyes, when they opened, were the colour of violets, fringed with two rows of thick black lashes.

Elizabeth Rosemond Taylor was born in Hampstead, London on February 27, 1932, the second child of Francis Taylor, an art dealer, and his wife Sara Sothern, a former actress. The Taylors were American middle-class, from Kansas. Mrs Taylor had given up a promising acting career when she married, but her professional instincts merely went into cold storage years later they would be the driving force behind her daughter's career.

The Taylor children were absorbed into an atmosphere of money and love. But, even at an early age, Elizabeth was prone to more ailments than most children suffer — a hint perhaps, of the appalling succession of illnesses she would later endure as an adult. Her nanny, Frieda Gill, was particularly responsible for introducing acting to her. When Elizabeth was two years old, she and Howard were encouraged to perform little improvised plays for their **parents'** tea time. The fantasy world immediately won favour with the little girl — acting had arrived in her life. A year later her ballet teacher arranged a dance recital at which the guests of honour were the Duchess of York and her daughters, the Princesses Elizabeth and Margaret Rose.

Early in 1939, Americans living in England were advised to go home: war with Germany seemed inevitable and reluctantly, the Taylors prepared to return. Elizabeth was seven when they arrived in Pasadena, California — a little English girl, conditioned by the environment in which she had flourished. She was deeply distressed at leaving the home and country she loved. Elizabeth was tiny and beautiful and she spoke with an English accent — it was a combination to promote envy. The Taylor children were different from their American counterparts and as a result they were ostracised. I was probably Elizabeth's first experience of rejection and disapproval: later, when her life became public property, she was to experience it again, many times.

Opposite: with Greer Garson in Julia Misbehaves

Francis Taylor opened an art gallery in Hollywood sensing that the movie executives might welcome a little culture. He and his wife bought a house overlooking the Pacific. It just happened to be an area populated by the most powerful men in the film industry and the children with whom Elizabeth and Howard played were the offspring of those powerful people. The appearance of Elizabeth Taylor was not unnoticed. It was the era of child stars and Mrs Taylor encouraged her daughter's artistic development with piano and singing lessons. Metro-Goldwyn-Mayer, at that time the most celebrated film studio, with its formidable stable of stars, became aware of Elizabeth and auditioned her. Louis B Mayer urged his people to sign her, but Mrs Taylor had already arranged another audition with Universal and it was the latter company which signed Elizabeth to a year's contract.

The first film involved three days work on *There's One Born Every Minute*, followed by a short, *Man or Mouse* with 'Alfalfa', which was never imported to Britain. Then Universal forgot about her. The contract was not renewed.

In 1942 Elizabeth began her association with Metro-Goldwyn-Mayer. The studio would become an important influence in her life and, under their guidance, Elizabeth Taylor would become a household name, a superstar. They would carefully manipulate her as they did all their stars. When an unwise romance threatened, they would send her off to make a film somewhere else. When their influence waned, they would adapt and make the best of it. But, in Elizabeth's case, the manipulation cannot be said to have been harmful. It was benevolent control, always benign, usually for her own good. The credit for this probably belongs to the fact that Elizabeth had parents who were concerned and watchful of their daughter's future. Francis and Sara Taylor were determined that, even though their daughter was an actress, her personal happiness came first.

The impact Elizabeth made in her first film for Metro-Goldwyn-Mayer, *Lassie Come Home*, ensured that they were not making a mistake. On her first day on that picture, she handled a horse with such assurance that her name was noted down for another property Metro had been having difficulty casting – *National Velvet*. Between the two she made a small appearance in *Jane Eyre*, as the little girl at Lowood School who befriends Jane and dies young; and she

Opposite: with Michael Wilding and Michael Junior.

played Irene Dunne's daughter in *The White Cliffs of Dover*. But it was *National Velvet* that made Elizabeth Taylor a star. Producer Pandro Berman wanted someone taller than this little ten year-old. Elizabeth started eating more and every day she presented herself to his office to be measured until finally she achieved the required height. To this day, the notches measuring her growth rate over this period of three months are still to be seen on the wall.

Elizabeth's adolescence was spent almost exclusively in fantasyland. She wrote a book about a pet chipmunk, called "Nibbles and Me", which was excellent publicity. At the studio she was loved and cherished. At fourteen she had Howard Hughes in hot pursuit. But boys her own age, Howard's friends, left her severely alone. She was beautiful, she was famous and she was often quite lonely. The romantic life of Elizabeth Taylor was still a thing of the future.

But Metro did not really know how to use her as an adolescent and she made a number of forgettable films. She was spiteful Amy in *Little Women*, under a ludicrous wig of blonde curls, and at sixteen played Robert Taylor's wife in the British production, *Conspirator*.

The first serious love of Elizabeth's life happened when she was sixteen. She met Glenn Davis, all-American hero of West Point, soon on his way to the Korean War. It was the kind of romance the studio — and the newspapers — were eager to encourage. Her mother also encouraged it. She said, "I felt Elizabeth's seeing Glenn Davis was so normal. He was such a football hero and every young girl in America was crazy about him. I never worried about what would be the outcome. I thought when he returned from Korea she would have outgrown it." As soon as Glenn left for Korea, Elizabeth left for England to make *Conspirator*. Every day she wrote adoring letters to her hero, every day he wrote to her. But by the time he returned from Korea, Mrs Taylor's prediction came true: he was out of Elizabeth's orbit. In England she became infatuated with an older man — Michael Wilding, later to become her second husband. There she was, playing the wife of Robert Taylor for a film, and off-set continuing her school lessons. The irony of the situation was not lost on Elizabeth.

Wilding said at the time: "She was very lovely and very busy. She was working. She was studying. She was writing to her soldier boy, and among other things she was going to balls. Lord Mountbatten gave one for his daughter, Pamela, and on

Opposite: visiting B J Simmons, the London costumiers

that occasion I was very aware of young Miss Taylor dancing with Prince Philip. I managed – I found myself compelled to manage – to see her during the lulls."

The following year – 1950 – saw the successful situation comedy *Father of the Bride* with Elizabeth as the daughter of Spencer Tracy and Joan Bennett; the formula was repeated in the next year's sequel, *Father's Little Dividend*. The first film which gave her any leeway as an actress – in fact the first film Elizabeth considers as a challenge – was George Stevens' *A Place In The Sun*. This adaptation of "An American Tragedy" cast her as the beautiful socialite who becomes involved with an ambitious loser, George Eastman, played with all his intense skill by Montgomery Clift. Stevens was the first director to rate Elizabeth as an actress and he later had more cause to be proud of her when they worked together again. Variety said of her performance: "For Miss Taylor, at least, the histrionics are of a quality so far beyond anything she has done previously that Stevens must be credited with a minor miracle."

She and Clift had a very close relationship lasting until Clift's death. In many ways he was unlike any other man in her life: he was constant but he was unpredictable.

It was after *A Place In The Sun* was finished that Elizabeth Taylor met Nicky Hilton, son and heir of Conrad Hilton, owner of the hotel chain. On Christmas Day, 1949, Nicky Hilton asked Francis Taylor's permission to marry his daughter. Five weeks later, Elizabeth graduated from the University High School in Los Angeles. That night Nicky and Elizabeth celebrated at a nightclub. "Your heart knows when you meet the right man, doesn't it? There's no doubt in my mind that Nick is the one I want to spend my life with. We met last October and we've never had one moment of misunderstanding." So an excited Elizabeth told Louella Parsons, the gossip columnist. Years later the quote would still haunt her.

On May 5, 1950 Elizabeth Rosemond Taylor married Conrad Nicholson Hilton Jnr at the Church of the Good Shepherd before a congregation of 550 people. Outside, over 3,000 fans clamoured for a sight of her and policemen had to restrain them. It was a picture book occasion. Afterwards she and Nicky were to leave for a lengthy honeymoon, the gift of Elizabeth's new father-in-law. The wedding was beautiful, but the marriage was unofficially declared a disaster before the honeymoon ended. Elizabeth Taylor divorced Nicky Hilton on January 26, 1951 on the grounds of mental cruelty. She

Opposite: off set during the making of Rhapsody

was still only eighteen. Metro-Goldwyn-Mayer put her into a film, obviously thinking that work would cure her. The title was, ironically, *Love Is Better Than Ever*, and although the director was Stanley Donen it was not much of a film. A costume drama — *Ivanhoe* — brought her back to England but professionally it was hardly worth the trip.

Private life was another matter. One of the first people who contacted her was Michael Wilding. The Taylor-Wilding marriage was probably the most friendly of Elizabeth's life. Wilding was an older man, an established actor in England. He understood about wine and food and he cherished this beautiful girl, although he appreciated the folly of the relationship. Anna Neagle was Elizabeth's bridesmaid and the wedding took place at Caxton Hall. Again there was a mob anxious for a glimpse of Elizabeth. "I hope you will all be as happy some day as I am right this moment," she announced. "This is, for me, the beginning of a happy end." The Wildings honeymooned in the Swiss Alps and then returned to England.

When Metro-Goldwyn-Mayer recalled her to America for a film, they offered her husband a contract. However Elizabeth had news of her own. She was pregnant. She and Michael were ecstatic: they bought a house in the Hollywood hills — to the west was the Santa Monica mountains and the Pacific; to the north the snow-capped Sierras. On January 7, 1953 Michael Howard Wilding was born by Caesarian section. Elizabeth was in hospital for five weeks and even after she was allowed home the nurses had to be in constant attendance. The first day she was allowed out of bed was her twenty-first birthday, February 27, 1953. But Elizabeth Taylor's maternal instinct was fired: everything to do with motherhood enchanted her. That she had great difficulty having children did not lessen her need for them. The first time Elizabeth was pregnant, she made no secret of it and was immediately put on suspension by the studio. The second time she kept quiet until her condition was obvious. The reason was simple — she needed the money. Christopher Edward Wilding was born on Elizabeth's twenty-third birthday. She was warned then that to attempt motherhood again might be fatal.

She was loaned to Paramount in 1954 to replace Vivien Leigh in *Elephant Walk*, but since scenes with Miss Leigh had already been shot and the studio did not want the additional cost of re-shooting, Elizabeth was required to match Vivien

Opposite: publicity still during the making of Cynthia

Leigh exactly. She did not enjoy the film. Another costume
drama — *Beau Brummell* — and the light-weight *The Last
Time I Saw Paris* also highlighted the fact that Metro did not
know how to tap the talent of Elizabeth Taylor.

During these years, when the indifferent films outflanked the
memorable ones, there were only two directors who truly
believed in her. One was George Stevens. The other was
Richard Brooks who directed her in *The Last Time I Saw
Paris*. "What impressed me was that the real Elizabeth was
not the publicity figure that had been created. She had a
knack of looking at herself in two lights — at what she was
supposed to be according to the press, but also with the
honesty and cynicism that comes from disappointment. Her
disappointment was that she was not regarded as an actress,
but merely as a beautiful girl."

Again George Stevens came to her rescue. He borrowed her
for *Giant*. It was a testing role in many ways — she had to
age from young girl to grand-mother, and although the later
scenes were a big challenge to both Elizabeth and her co-star
Rock Hudson, who played her husband, the film was an
imaginative and worthy adaptation of the massive Edna
Ferber novel. George Stevens recalls: "Elizabeth had been
associating with older people all her life, and there was a
great maturity about her. But when she reported for *Giant*,
I saw she had managed to maintain the youthfulness that had
been part of her make-up when she had been on the
borderline of being a teenager.

"There I was asking her to play long scenes that had to do
with the heroine's grandchildren. Imagine, at that time of her
life. She did it. She got hold of it. So did Rock. They were
playing scenes way beyond their years, but they made it
work." Playing Elizabeth's children were Carroll Baker and
Dennis Hopper.

Towards the end of shooting Elizabeth became ill, and when
co-star James Dean died, she became so hysterical that
Stevens had to shoot round her for two days. But,
professionally, she had not been used so well since *A Place In
The Sun*.

Actor Kevin McCarthy was responsible for Elizabeth Taylor
meeting the man who was to change her lifestyle, as well as
give her confidence in her acting ability — Mike Todd. Todd,
showman *extraordinaire* turned film-maker with *Around The
World in Eighty Days*. He lived in the most wildly
extravagant style and he was, without doubt, the most

Opposite: with John Ericson in Rhapsody

exciting and different man Elizabeth had ever met. On June 30, 1956 when Michael and Elizabeth Wilding stepped aboard Mike Todd's yacht for a champagne reception, it was the end of the Wilding marriage. They remained friends: Wilding later attended the marriage of Elizabeth Taylor and Mike Todd and, even further in the future, became Richard Burton's agent. Few divorces have been conducted in so civilised an atmosphere.

Elizabeth flew off on location for *Raintree County* with her old friend Montgomery Clift (a changed Clift, though, following that disastrous car smash after an evening with the Wildings). From New York, Mike Todd wooed Elizabeth lavishly — with phone calls, with daily deliveries of jewels. He treated her with an extravagance she found completely captivating. "Over those five weeks of phone calls, Mike Todd and I came really to know one another. I had never in all my life talked as I did with him."

Raintree County, directed by Edward Dmytryk, was a happy film to make, although some critics found her performance as a southern belle unconvincing. It won her an Oscar nomination and made a great deal of money.

Elizabeth Taylor married Mike Todd on February 3, 1957 in Acalpulco in a Jewish ceremony. Eddie Fisher was best man, his wife Debbie Reynolds and Elizabeth's sister-in-law, Mara Taylor, were the bridesmaids. One of Mike Todd's little extravagances was to give his wife a present every Saturday — because they had been married on a Saturday. They were seldom apart. Then Elizabeth announced that she was pregnant and Mike Todd worried her doctors mercilessly for progress reports. The baby was due in November but on August 6 the doctors decided they could wait no longer. Liza Todd was born, weighing just four pounds and not breathing. For fifteen minutes she was kept alive by artificial respiration. Then she began to breathe. Asked whether his daughter was as beautiful as her mother Mike Todd replied: "Compared to Liza her mother looks like Frankenstein."

Elizabeth was told that on no account could she have any more children. Mike Todd believed utterly in Elizabeth's power as an actress. The notices she received for *Gaint* seemed to confirm it, but Elizabeth would not attend the premiere and was determined to retire. Then she was offered *Cat On a Hot Tin Roof* and Mike desperately wanted her to do it. More than anything, he wanted her to win an Oscar. The film had to be a winner and she caught Todd's

Opposite: with Finlay Currie in Ivanhoe

nthusiasm. The film was based on a Tennessee Williams play
ith Paul Newman, Burl Ives and Judith Anderson as co-stars
nd Richard Brooks directing. Brooks said on the first day:
When we started working I realised how much Elizabeth had
rown. She had a new confidence in herself. She was more
ree to express herself as an actress. She was poised and not
n trial anymore."

)n March 22, 1958 Mike Todd was to be named "Showman
f the Year" in New York. He arranged to fly there in his
rivate plane, The Lucky Liz. Elizabeth pleaded to be
llowed to go with him but she had a cold and a temperature
f 102 degrees. Todd knew how a cold could develop into
omething much more serious with Elizabeth, and there was
o question that he would let her go. Outside a gale raged.
irk Douglas turned down his invitation to accompany him.
oseph Mankiewicz also refused. Mike Todd rang his wife
ust before take-off. It was their last conversation. A week
fter *Cat on a Hot Tin Roof* began shooting, Mike Todd was
ead. Elizabeth Taylor had discovered early in her life that
he price of fame was to lose any claim on privacy. Joy must
e shared: so must grief. Faced with the void which Mike
Todd's death left in her life, she could not escape the curious,
ager to see how a star faced bereavement. Mike Todd's
uneral was an ordeal she shared not only with family and
riends but with vast hordes of the public. It was a horrifying
xperience. As the casket was lowered into the ground
Elizabeth seemed to realise what was happening and,
suddenly coming out of her glazed trance, she flung herself
nto the casket crying, "Oh, no, no, no! Mike! Mike you
cannot leave me here alone."

The weeping woman was led away, but it took many
sedatives to calm her. It was during the desperate days that
followed that Elizabeth Taylor gained some strength from
Mike Todd's faith, and she decided to convert. It was not a
new idea. During Todd's lifetime Elizabeth had studied the
Jewish faith but he never pressed her, saying that a
conversion must be totally her decision.

Three weeks later Elizabeth went on the set to see how
things were going. "We were doing one of the scenes where
Burl Ives, as Big Daddy, first realises he may be dying," said
Brooks. "It was too late for me to change anything. I didn't
know how such a scene would affect Elizabeth, but I
decided the gamble was better than my turning her down. So
I arranged for the set to be closed to all outsiders and I told

Opposite: her Oscar-winning appearance in Butterfield 8

the cast she was arriving. I knew it would be hard on all of u
The crew was handpicked from a group she had worked wit
since her childhood. She loved them and they loved her.

"All we could do was play it by ear. We were shooting as sh
came in, after lunch and we went right on, which wasn'
easy. She was very pale, shockingly thin. But she didn'
break down and the actors continued."

She went back to work and, although it was painful, the film
was a credit to her and her performance was remarkable. I
won her another Oscar nomination. Elizabeth's next film wa
another big success, *Suddenly Last Summer* with
Montgomery Clift. She played a girl on the brink of madness
The director, Joseph Mankiewicz, described her as "The
Grandma Moses of acting." One of the scenes involved wa
a twelve-page monologue which ended with Elizabeth rolling
on the floor, screaming hysterically. Apparently, so good wa
her performance that the English crew, normally restrained in
such circumstances, broke into involuntary cheers.

Eddie Fisher, who had been Mike Todd's closest friend
helped Elizabeth over this crisis period. He took her to
dinner, he sang to her. He made her feel alive again. When
Debbie Reynolds divorced him, the world was swift to blame
Elizabeth Taylor. The truth was that the Fisher marriage wa
over long before Eddie's involvement with Elizabeth. Publi
sympathy was totally with Debbie and, however justified i
may have been, Elizabeth's chances of winning an Oscar fo
Cat On A Hot Tin Roof were as good as over. Hollywood
does not always only give Oscars for good performances –
many have been won on sympathy, or for good behaviour
or withheld for bad behaviour. Later Elizabeth would win a
sympathy Oscar for *Butterfield 8*, but she virtually had to
die for it.

Eddie Fisher said: "I know I am not the great love in
Elizabeth's life, but she is the great love of mine." They
were married on May 12, 1959 in a Jewish ceremony with
Mike Todd Jnr as the best man. Elizabeth worked and Eddie
looked after Elizabeth. 20th Century-Fox began making
stupendous offers for Elizabeth to play Cleopatra. She
refused and the price got higher. However one picture
remained in her Metro-Goldwyn-Mayer contract –
Butterfield 8. She didn't want to do it and was as difficult as
she could be: "Nothing you can say will make me like this
film and nothing you can do will make me want to play it,"
she told the director. She had no option: Metro insisted. She

Opposite: in Hammersmith Is Ou

made extortionist demands and the studio met every one of them. However, much as she hated the film, it won her that Oscar she'd been chasing all her career. "I knew my performance hadn't deserved it, that it was a sympathy award."

The story is told that when the offers for *Cleopatra* were going higher and higher, Elizabeth relayed a message through Eddie: "Tell them I'll do it for a million." Even she, long accustomed to extravagance, didn't believe it possible. It was. She arrived in London on September 8, 1960. Peter Finch was to play Caesar, Stephen Boyd was to play Mark Antony and the picture would be directed by Rouben Mamoulian. Then fate played its hand. Elizabeth was continually ill, usually with minor ailments which developed complications. 'Flu turned to pneumonia and, once recovered, Elizabeth needed time to recuperate. The insurance companies urged the producers to select another Cleopatra. Walter Wanger refused: With half a million already spent, three central characters changed: Mamoulian, Finch and Boyd. In mid-January they reassembled in London. Joseph Mankiewicz was hired to direct and co-write; Rex Harrison would play Caesar and Richard Burton would be Mark Antony. The location was switched from London to Rome. But before they could get started, Elizabeth faced her biggest fight. On February 26 she was in bed with another cold. Within a few hours she had lobar pneumonia and specialists rushed her to the London Clinic. Rumours circled the globe that Elizabeth Taylor was dying. It was true. A tracheotomy was performed to enable her to breathe. Her temperature was 108 degrees. "When I was unconscious and dying, I felt I touched God, I had no time to pray. I just cried 'Oh God, help me.' I screamed to God and He heard me," she said later.

Hundreds of people waited for news outside the Clinic, and later, when the battle was won, her doctor spoke to the press. "Out of every hundred who have Miss Taylor's type of pneumonia, rarely do two survive. On four occasions Miss Taylor was as near to death as she could be. Her courage and will power pulled her through."

Late in September 1961 Elizabeth Taylor, Eddie Fisher and their entourage arrived in Rome to make *Cleopatra*. Opinions vary about the first words between Elizabeth Taylor and Richard Burton. In the book "Richard Burton" by Fergus Cashin and John Cottrell it is recalled that Burton said, "Has anybody told you that you're a very pretty girl?" In

Opposite: in Boom!

"Elizabeth Taylor" by Ruth Waterbury Elizabeth is reported as saying, "Hello, Dickie," (knowing Burton hated being called Dick) to which he responded, "Hello Liz" (knowing that she hated being called Liz). Probably even the principals have forgotten the accurate word-for-word transcript. In any case, they had met before, during Elizabeth's marriage to Michael Wilding.

In Rome, for the first few months, Burton had little to do. Because the script was being written as they went along, the film was shot in sequence, a virtually unheard-of luxury in film-making. So Elizabeth played most of her early scenes with Rex Harrison. In any case she and Eddie Fisher were busy adopting a little girl, Maria, through a German agency suggested to them by actress Maria Schell (for whom they named their daughter). Once Elizabeth Taylor and Richard Burton began their scenes together the unit became aware that the emotion was no mere act for the cameras. "She looks at you with those eyes and your blood churns," Burton told a visiting British journalist. The following Sunday this information was digested along with the coffee and cornflakes, and love among the Pyramids became front page news. The denials, the counter denials, the to-ing and fro-ing with Rome and *Cleopatra* as its core continued for months. The publicity department were kept more busy issuing official statements than with publicising the film: not that publicity was altogether necessary. The headlines assured that this most famous of subjects would not pass unnoticed into the cinemas.

Elizabeth Taylor finally took off Mike Todd's wedding ring, the ring she had worn all during her marriage to Eddie Fisher. *Cleopatra* was finished on July 11, 1962, the most expensive and lengthy film of all time. Perhaps, in retrospect, it was not as bad a film as it was judged to be. While it did have its dull patches, it was not a negligible performance from Elizabeth Taylor. She looked spectacular and, certainly in the first half — Caesar's half — gave a credible performance of some depth. The second half can probably only now be viewed with any impartiality: at the time it was like a peepshow. Even the advertising campaign accentuated this by showing Taylor and Burton reclining lovingly. Only later, when he threatened court action, was Harrison's Caesar painted into the poster, peeping around the purple curtains. But it was Harrison who won the warm reviews. The New Statesman's review was among the most cutting about Elizabeth:

"Monotony in a split skirt, a pre-Christian Elizabeth Arden with sequinned eyelids and occasions constantly too large for her. Plumply pretty, she gives herself womanfully to the impersonation of the world's prime seductress, yet nary a spark flies."

On December 7, 1962 Elizabeth Taylor and Richard Burton arrived in London. Elizabeth and her entourage were installed at the Dorchester Hotel. Burton also had a suite there. Sybil Burton and their two daughters were in Hampstead. Elizabeth and Richard had become well used to being attacked in print. If anything, it served to strengthen the basic relationship. While everyone took sides — including friends and family — the Burton/Taylor liaison became more and more permanent.

Cunningly cashing in on the situation was Metro-Goldwyn-Mayer who hired Elizabeth and Richard to make *The VIPs*, playing husband and wife, and got the film out before *Cleopatra* had been generally seen. *The VIPs* was a lovely, glossy wallow of a film, with screenplay by Terence Rattigan and direction by Anthony Asquith. Elizabeth was dressed by Givenchy and the action took place at London Airport where fog grounds aircraft, thus causing

with Jane Powell in A Date With Judy

repercussions in several people's lives. There was a fascination about seeing these famous illicit lovers playing husband and wife although the late lamented Margaret Rutherford stole every scene she appeared in as the lovably eccentric Duchess of Brighton.

In April 1963 Sybil Burton announced a formal separation. The following year, on March 15 in Montreal, Elizabeth Taylor and Richard Burton were married. "I'm so happy you can't believe it," Elizabeth said. "You don't know what this means to me to be married privately and without a terrible crush." Richard made do with a Shakespeare quote: "There will be no more marriages."

The Burtons' professional partnership achieved varying degrees of success. They obviously believed that the couple that work together stay together. When a role for Elizabeth could not be found in a Burton film, she seemed content to sit on the side of the set and watch him work. But in spite of the apparent waning of her ambition she did some of her best work during this period, although not in the disappointingly soppy *The Sandpiper*, directed by Vincente Minnelli, with Elizabeth as a bohemian artist who has an affair with a married priest (Burton). It was shot on location

with Ava Gardner in The Blue Bird of Happiness

in the picturesque Big Sur area of the Pacific coast and looked enchanting. They more than redeemed themselves with *Who's Afraid of Virginia Woolf?* Mike Nichols' stunning film based on Edward Albee's play which little by little peels away the layers of a marriage. It was memorably played by the four members of the cast and Elizabeth Taylor was at last acknowledged as one of the great actresses of her generation. The film also broke new ground with its dialogue — words never uttered on celluloid before were shouted and bawled. The film won for Elizabeth her second Best Actress Oscar, this time for a performance, not sympathy. It was the first time she had been seen as a battered old hag, overweight, shrill of voice, and with grey hair.

Flushed with success, the Burtons continued with one of the most appealing adaptations of a Shakespeare play — *The Taming of the Shrew*, the directing debut of Franco Zeffirelli. It was an exquisitely beautiful film to look at and not unfaithful to the text. Elizabeth made a fiery, passionate Katharina and the film was chosen as the Royal Film. For once the Royals probably had an enjoyable night at the movies.

Elizabeth had a cameo part as Helen of Troy in *Doctor Faustus*, the less-than-successful adaptation of the Christopher Marlowe tragedy in which Richard Burton played the title role. Her next film was grossly underrated at the time — *Reflections in a Golden Eye*, John Huston's shadowy tale of corruption and marriage. Originally intended for Montgomery Clift, the film was finally made with Marlon Brando in the Clift role. Elizabeth simmered and simpered as the frustrated, teasing wife and Brando as her homosexual husband was excellent.

The Comedians, which followed, was set in Haiti with Elizabeth as an Ambassador's wife having an affair on the side, with the island's unhappy political situation as the background. Based on a fascinating Graham Greene novel, the film lost some of the original's potency, but was still enormously watchable. Peter Ustinov played her husband, Burton her lover. Joseph Losey's *Boom!* was a commercial flop, but Elizabeth looked magnificent. Considering that it was based on a Tennessee Williams play "The Milk Train Doesn't Stop Here Anymore" and that Elizabeth has enjoyed great success in Williams' work, it is surprising that the film attracted so little interest. Another Losey film, the strange *Secret Ceremony*, with Elizabeth as a whore and Mia Farrow as a young girl who imagines she is Miss Taylor's daughter,

also failed to capture audiences. After this Elizabeth renewed her working relationship with George Stevens making *The Only Game in Town* in Paris, while Richard Burton made *Staircase*. Both films were made in Paris for tax reasons although *The Only Game in Town* was supposedly set in Las Vegas. Here Warren Beatty played her gambling lover. The film was made in difficult conditions, since Elizabeth was suffering with her back most of the time. Even so, the subject was not the stuff on which reputations were made and it was a pity that Stevens and Elizabeth, whose joint efforts were previously fine, should have come to this slight tale.

In *Under Milk Wood* she played a small role as Rosie Probert and then, again with Richard Burton, she made *Hammersmith is Out* playing a common blonde barmaid while Burton glowered his way through the role of the madman. It was moderately well received. But *Zee & Co*, while not restoring her to the level of *Who's Afraid of Virginia Woolf?*, nor yet to that of *Reflections in a Golden Eye*, was an interesting bravura performance with Elizabeth as Zee Blakely married to Michael Caine and determined, by fair means or foul, to keep her husband when he strays to the calmer arms of Stella (Susannah York). Generally it was felt that Margaret Leighton stole the film as party-giver Gladys, but Elizabeth raved and ravaged her way through.

The marriage to Richard Burton — fiery, eventful — seemed good and strong and enduring. Elizabeth's health continued to be a great source of anxiety — in a recent interview she revealed that she had thirty operations in her life. She once asked her doctor whether she was accident-prone. "If you were," he replied, "you wouldn't still be here."

In 1971 Elizabeth's elder son, Michael Wilding Jnr married at Caxton Hall and quite naturally it was Elizabeth who got the press coverage. In 1972 she reached the critical age of forty. A lavish party was held in Budapest where Richard was making a film. There were vague mutterings in the press about extravagance but the Burtons salved their conscience by giving a similar amount of money to UNICEF. Friends flew in from everywhere.

Elizabeth then made *Nightwatch*, a rather silly film about a woman who may or may not have witnessed a murder in the house at the bottom of her garden. It hardly seemed to matter. It was the last film of Laurence Harvey, a close of Elizabeth's. She played his wife, neurotic Ellen Wheeler, subject to visions. Billie Whitelaw played the other woman. Both this and *Zee & Co* were directed by Brian G Hutton.

Opposite: with Richard Burton in The Sandpiper

In *Ash Wednesday*, Elizabeth played a frumpish, gone-to-seed middle-aged woman who undergoes overall cosmetic surgery to win back the love of her errent husband, played by Henry Fonda. Once rejuvenated, she turns into the ravishing Elizabeth Taylor of old and wins the transitory affection of some beautiful young men (notably Helmut Berger) but alas, not that of her husband. The shock of the first ten minutes and the nauseating glimpses of an actual operation were fascinating, but the glossy improbability of the rest made it a less than satisfactory film.

Identikit, based on Muriel Spark's novel "The Driver's Seat" starred Elizabeth as a woman searching for the man who is trying to destroy her, and, at the time of writing has still not been taken up for British distribution although it was made in 1974. Following that she was persuaded by Jack Haley Jnr to join her former MGM contract colleagues to link the musical footage in *That's Entertainment*. A collage of the most memorable musical numbers from the rich archives of MGM, it gave audiences of the '70s an orgy of nostalgia and as the advertising noted, "Boy do we need it now."

There was a six-month separation from Richard Burton, followed by a much publicised reconciliation. This did not last, however, and in June 1974 Elizabeth Taylor and Richard Burton were divorced. It was a numbing experience for their fans: the couple that seemed absolutely right for each other, the lifestyle that from the outside looked so ravishingly exotic, finally crumbled to nothing. In the wake of her divorce from Burton, Elizabeth went to Russia to make *The Bluebird*, an American-Russian co-production directed by George Kukor with a mixed nationality crew. A musical based on the turn of the century metaphysical idyll by Maurice Maeterlinck, Elizabeth was cast in twin roles as the Fairy Berylune and Light. Although 20th Century-Fox have the distribution for Britain, the film is taking a long while to appear.

Elizabeth was again reunited with Richard Burton when the film ended. They remarried in October 1975 in Botswana, near the Rhodesian border. The ceremony was performed by the local District Commissioner. They divorced a second time in 1976 and Richard married Suzy Hunt, ex-wife of British motor racing driver James Hunt.

The new man in Elizabeth's life was John Warner, a politician and former US Secretary of the Navy, whom she married on December 4, 1976 at his estate in the Blue Ridge Mountains

Opposite: with Warren Beatty in The Only Game in Town

In Suddenly Last Summer

In Cynthia

of Virginia. She had just returned from Vienna where she made another musical, *A Little Night Music*, based on the Stephen Sondheim musical play. Elizabeth played Desirée, Hermione Gingold recreated her role of Madame Armfeldt and Diana Rigg co-starred as the aristocratic Countess Charlotte. The casting of Elizabeth caused some consternation among devotees of the play and many wondered how she would cope with singing the Sondheim standard, "Send in the Clowns," which properly belongs to Glynis Johns, who played Desirée on Broadway. The Taylor version was, in fact, rather good.

Following this, Elizabeth made a guest appearance in *Victory at Entebbe*, the made-for-television version of the daring Israeli rescue operation in Uganda in 1976. Elizabeth and Kirk Douglas played the parents of Linda Blair, one of the hostages. This version was shown theatrically outside America where it just beat *Raid on Entebbe* to the theatres, but was eclipsed in the notices.

Her ambition next appeared to be centred round John Warner and a role quite new to her: politician's wife. "I could sit and listen to John for hours, he's a dream," she said. "First of all he can tell better stories than I can. He has a better sense of humour than I have. And he's even got more money

This page: with Mickey Rooney in National Velvet

Opposite: with Jeanette MacDonald off set in Cynthia

than I have! He makes me feel ten years younger, he's s
intelligent, tender and loving. I'm so happy." She bega
addressing women's luncheons in order to boost he
husband's career and she dispensed with her hairdressers
secretary, wardrobe mistress and general retinue for the firs
time since she became a star actress. Nevertheless the coupl
announced their separation in December of 1981.

During the marriage she made just one film, *The Mirro
Crack'd*, and that only because the comparatively shor
shooting schedule would not interfere with the idyll o
organised married life. It was derived from one of Agatha
Christie's Miss Marple stories (the lady sleuth was played by
Angela Lansbury) and cast Elizabeth as an over-the-hill film
star making a comeback in a film drama about Elizabeth 1
and Mary Queen of Scots. Then murder takes over from the
fictional drama … Guy Hamilton directed the film in British
country locations familiar to Elizabeth from her childhood.
Her co-stars included Kim Novak, Tony Curtis, Rock
Hudson and Geraldine Chaplin.

This page: with Larry Parks in The Light Fantastic

Once again between marriages, her career may yet enter a
new phase. One can only wish her the happiness she has
earned — and the epitaph she has requested: "Here lies
Elizabeth Taylor. Thank you for every moment good and
bad. I've enjoyed it all."

FILMOGRAPHY

'MAN OR MOUSE (US 1942)
A short film produced by Universal. No GB distribution.
With: Carl 'Alfalfa' Switzer, Elizabeth Taylor

THERE'S ONE BORN EVERY MINUTE (US 1942)
Director/Harold Young. GB distribution/General Films
Certificate U. 60 mins.
With: Hugh Herbert, Tom Brown, Peggy Moran
Lemuel P Twine (Herbert Lom) runs a pudding factory with
the help of his family. Twine's lifestyle is dramatically
changed when a laboratory discovers that his pudding
contain Vitamin Z. Elizabeth Taylor made her debut film
appearance as Gloria, the youngest member of the Twine
family in this comedy directed by Harold Young.

LASSIE COME HOME (US 1943)
Dir/Fred M Wilcox. Scr/Hugo Butler. Technicolor. GB
distribution/Metro-Goldwyn-Mayer. Certificate U. 89 mins.
With: Roddy McDowall (Joe), Donald Crisp (Sam), Edmund
Gwenn (Rowlie Palmer), Elizabeth Taylor (Priscilla), Lassie
The first and certainly the best of the Lassie films, this was
also Elizabeth Taylor's first film for MGM. The story is that of
a poor family who, unable to make ends meet any longer, are
forced to sell their dog. Elizabeth Taylor plays Priscilla, the
young grand-daughter of the Duke of Rudling (Nigel Bruce),
Lassie's new owner. After making several attempts to escape,
the dog is finally helped by Priscilla who feels sympathy for
the animal's unhappiness and yearning to return home.

JANE EYRE (US 1943)
Dir/Robert Stevenson. GB distribution/20th Century-Fox.
Certificate A. 97 mins.
With: Orson Welles, Joan Fontaine
Taylor makes an unbilled appearance as the little girl at
Lowood School who befriends the young orphan Jane Eyre,
only to die at an early age. Based on Charlotte Brontë's classic
novel, Joan Fontaine played the adult Jane; Orson Welles
was the brooding Rochester.

THE WHITE CLIFFS OF DOVER (US 1944)
Dir/Clarence Brown. Scr/Claudine West, Jan Lustwig,
George Froeschel, based on the poem 'The White Cliffs' by
Opposite: in Alice Duer Miller. Ph/George Folsey. GB distribution/
Julia Metro-Goldwyn-Mayer. Certificate U. 124 mins.
Misbehaves

With: Irene Dunne, Alan Marshall, Roddy McDowall, Peter Lawford
Taylor made another brief uncredited appearance as Irene Dunne's young daughter in this wartime tearjerker about an American girl who marries into English aristocracy and loses her husband in World War I and her son in World War II.

NATIONAL VELVET (US 1945)
Dir/Clarence Brown. Scr/Theodore Reeves, Helen Deutsch, based on the novel by Enid Bagnold. Ph/Leonard Smith. Technicolor.   GB   distribution/Metro-Goldwyn-Mayer. Certificate U. 123 mins.
With: Mickey Rooney (Mi), Donald Crisp (Mr Brown), Elizabeth Taylor (Velvet Brown), Angela Lansbury (Edwina Brown), Anne Revere (Mrs Brown)
This is the film that made Elizabeth Taylor into a star, at the age of ten. The story is that of Mi Taylor, a former jockey who becomes friends with twelve year-old Velvet Brown (Taylor). When she wins a horse in a raffle, the young couple decide to train it in the hope of entering for the Grand National. As the day of the race nears, they must decide who will be the rider. Thought to be too short for the part Taylor was given three

This page: in Rhapsody

Opposite: with Larry Parks in The Light Fantastic

months to gain height and on the wall in producer Pandro Berman's office, the notches which he made daily to measure her growth rate, can still be seen.

COURAGE OF LASSIE (US 1946)

Dir/Fred M Wilcox. Scr/Lionel Houser. Ph/Leonard Smith. Technicolor. GB distribution/Metro-Goldwyn-Mayer. Certificate U. 92 mins.
With: Elizabeth Taylor (Kathie Merrick), Frank Morgan (Harry McBain), Tom Drake (Sgt Smithy), Lassie
In Taylor's second (and MGM's third) Lassie film, the collie gets drafted into the US Army in Europe when, after a road accident, the vet is unable to locate his owner. When the dog's nerves are shatterd by gun-fire he is sent back to America where, in a state of semi-wildness he kills chickens and becomes a nuisance to nearby farms. Taylor plays Kathie, who finds her long-lost companion and then has to battle against local ranchers when they obtain a court order to have the dog destroyed.

CYNTHIA (GB: THE RICH, FULL LIFE) (US 1947)

Dir/Robert Z Leonard. Music/Bronislau Kaper. GB distribution/Metro-Goldwyn-Mayer. Certificate U. 98 mins.
With: Elizabeth Taylor, George Murphy
An over-protected young girl of frail health (Taylor) finds a creative outlet in music and, after much harrassment from her parents (George Murphy and Mary Astor), is allowed to lead her own life and become independent.

LIFE WITH FATHER (US 1947)

Dir/Michael Curtis. Scr/Donald Ogden Stewart. Ph/Peverell Thurley, William V Skall. Technicolor. Music/Max Steiner. GB distribution/Warner. Certificate A. 111 mins.
With: Irene Dunne (Viviene O'Day), William Powell (Father O'Day), Elizabeth Taylor (Mary), Edmund Gwenn (Rev Dr Lloyd), Zasu Pitts (Cora)
Set in turn-of-the-century New York, the film stars William Powell and Irene Dunne as the parents of a family thrown into uproar when the father reveals he has never been baptised and never intends to be. This sudden revelation leaves his son Clarence (Jimmy Lydon), who is trying to woo and impress his girlfriend Mary (Taylor), distraught. He turns to his mother in the hope that she can change her husband's mind.

Opposite: with William Powell off set during The Girl Who Had Everything

A DATE WITH JUDY (US 1948)

Dir/Richard Thorpe. Scr/Dorothy Cooper, Dorothy Kingsley, based on characters created by Aleen Leslie. Ph/Robert Surtees. Technicolor. GB distribution / Metro-Goldwyn-Mayer. Certificate U. 113 mins.

With: Wallace Beery (Melvyn Colner Foster), Jane Powell (Judy Foster), Elizabeth Taylor (Carol Pringle), Carmen Miranda (Rosita Conchellas), Robert Stack (Stephen Andrews), Xavier Cugat and his Orchestra.

Taylor received third billing in this rather flat musical comedy about a teenager who suspects her friend of an illicit affair. MGM, still nurturing their new-found star, gave Taylor as much publicity as possible, and a press release of the time said: "Elizabeth Taylor is as British as they make them, and has more than enough talent to make her a favourite for the next decade. Watch her!"

JULIA MISBEHAVES (US 1948)

Dir/Jack Conway. Scr/William Ludwig, Harry Ruskin, Arthur Wimperis. Ph/Joseph Ruttenberg. GB distribution/Metro-Goldwyn-Mayer. Certificate A. 99 mins.

With: Greer Garson, Walter Pidgeon, Peter Lawford, Elizabeth Taylor.

Julia Packett, a down-on-her-luck music hall entertainer, receives an invitation to her daughter Susan's (Taylor) wedding. Julia has not seen her daughter, now eighteen, since she was a baby, when she separated from her husband (Walter Pidgeon). While performing at the theatre one night, Julia is spotted by her husband, whom Susan has secretly invited to the show, in an attempt to re-unite her parents.

LITTLE WOMEN (US 1949)

Dir/Mervyn Le Roy. Scr/Andrew Solt, Sarah Y Mason, Victor Heerman, based on the novel by Louisa May Alcott. Ph/Robert Planck, Charles Schoenbaum. Technicolor. Music/Adlolph Deutsch. GB distribution/Metro-Goldwyn-Mayer. Certificate U. 122 mins.

With: June Allyson (Jo), Peter Lawford, Margaret O'Brien (Beth), Janet Leigh (Meg), Elizabeth Taylor (Amy), Mary Astor (Marmee)

Under a wig of blonde curls, Taylor was cast as the spoiled Amy in this remake of the 1933 screen version of Louisa May Alcott's story of four sisters growing up in pre-civil War America. Focusing on their far-flung ambitions and romantic infatuations, this was a syrupy treatment of the story and paled considerably alongside the earlier version starring Katharine Hepburn and Joan Bennett.

CONSPIRATOR (US 1949)

Dir/Victor Saville. Scr/Sally Beson, Gerard Fairlie, based on the novel by Humphrey Slater. Ph/F A Young. Music/John Wooldridge. GB distribution/Metro-Goldwyn-Mayer. Certificate U. 87 mins.

With: Robert Taylor (Maj Michael Curragh), Elizabeth Taylor (Melinda Greyton), Robert Flemyng (Capt Hugh Ladholme), Honor Blackman (Joyce), Marie Ney (Lady Pennistone), Harold Warrender (Col Hammerbrook)

Elizabeth Taylor and Robert Taylor play husband and wife in this romantic melodrama directed by Victor Saville. Major Michael Curragh (Robert Taylor) appears to be a respectable military officer, but when his wife discovers that he is also an undercover Communist agent, she issues him with an ultimatum: he must give up either her or his political activities. Failing to do either, Curragh is horrifed to receive orders to liquidate his wife.

Opposite: in an MGM publicity shot

THE BIG HANGOVER (US 1949)

Prod-dir-scr/Norman Krasna. Ph/George Folsey. Music/ Adolph Deutch. GB distribution/Metro-Goldwyn-Mayer. Certificate U. 82 mins.

With: Van Johnson (David Maldon), Elizabeth Taylor (Mary Belney), Percy Waram (John Belney), Fay Holden (Martha Belney)

Following her romantic lead in *Conspirator*, this film marked the first of three successive Taylor comedies. The story concerns a young lawyer (Van Johnson) trying to get ahead with the higher echelons of his profession, but finding his task hampered by his allergy to drink. Mary Belney (Taylor) is the young lady he tries to woo in the process.

FATHER OF THE BRIDE (US 1950)

Prod/Pandro S Berman. Dir/Vincente Minnelli. Scr/Albert Hackett, Frances Goodrich, based on the novel by Edward Streeter. Ph/John Alton. Music/Adolph Deutch. GB distribution/Metro-Goldwyn-Mayer. Certificate U. 92 mins.

With: Spencer Tracy (Stanley Banks), Joan Bennett (Mrs Banks), Elizabeth Taylor (Kay), Don Taylor (Barclay Dunstone), Leo G Carroll (Caterer)

When Kay Banks (Taylor) announces to her mother (Joan

This page: with Brian Keith in Reflections in a Golden Eye

Opposite: another MGM publicity shot

Bennett) and father (Spencer Tracy) that she is going to get married, the entire household is thrown into a frenzy of activity. This gay and sprightly comedy saw Tracy in superb form as the father subjected to endless trials and tribulations during the days of preparation before the wedding. The film was a major success in 1950, and was released after Taylor's own wedding on May 5th to Conrad Nicholas Hilton Jnr, at which over 3,000 fans clamoured for a glimpse of the star.

FATHER'S LITTLE DIVIDEND (US 1951)
Prod/Pandro S Berman. Dir/Vincente Minnelli. Scr/Albert Hackett, Frances Goodrich, based on characters created by Edward Streeter. Ph/John Alton. GB distribution/Metro-Goldwyn-Mayer. Certificate U. 81 mins.
With: Spencer Tracy (Stanley Banks), Joan Bennett (Mrs Banks), Elizabeth Taylor (Kay), Don Taylor (Barclay Dunstone)
Using the original director (Vincente Minnelli) and cast, this sequel to *Father of the Bride* has young wife Taylor telling her parents that she is due to have a baby. Tracy is the expectant grandfather delighted for the newlyweds, but not entirely looking forward to the event.

A PLACE IN THE SUN (US 1951)
Prod-dir/George Stevens. Scr/Michael Wilson, Harry Brown, based on the novel 'An American Tragedy' by Theodore Drieser, and the Patrick Kearney play adapted from the novel. Ph/William C Mellor. GB distribution/Paramount. Certificate A. 122 mins.
With: Montgomery Clift (George Eastman), Shelley Winters (Alice Tripp), Elizabeth Taylor (Angela Vickers), Ann Reverse (Hannah Eastman), Raymond Burr (Marlowe)
Taylor was ecstatic about being cast opposite Montgomery Clift — then the hottest male acting property in Hollywood — for George Stevens' adaptation of the Theodore Dreiser's "An American Tragedy." This blunt indictment of the American dream and its corrupting influences cast Taylor as rich socialite Angela Vickers who falls in love with poor factory worker George Eastman (Clift), whom she meets at the home of his rich uncle. Shelley Winters plays the pathetic factory girl, Alice, who, after enjoying a brief affair with and becoming pregnant by Eastman, insists he marry her. Desperately seeking a way out of the dilemma, Eastman takes Alice boating, knowing she cannot swim ...

Opposite: with her baby Christopher Wilding

This page: with Richard Burton in Boom

LOVE IS BETTER THAN EVER (GB: THE LIGHT FANTASTIC) (US 1951)

Prod/William H Wright. Dir/Stanley Donen. Scr/Ruth Brooks Flipper. Ph/Harold Rosson. Music/Lennie Hayton. GB distribution/Metro-Goldwyn-Mayer. Certificate U. 81 mins.

With: Larry Parks (Jud Parker), Elizabeth Taylor (Anastasia Macaboy), Josephine Hutchinson (Mrs Macaboy), Tom Tully (Mr Macaboy)

This was a difficult film for Taylor to make, coming as it did in the wake of her divorce from Nicky Hilton. It was a disappointing comedy, directed by Stanley Donen. Larry Parks starred as talent agent Jud Parker trying to win the hand of Elizabeth Taylor as Anastasia Macaboy.

IVANHOE (GB 1952)

Prod/Padro S Berman. Dir/Richard Thorpe. Scr/Noel Langley, from Aeneas MacKenzie's adaptation of the novel by Sir Walter Scott. Ph/F A Young. Technicolor. Music/ Miklos Rozsa. GB distribution/Paramount. Certificate U. 107 mins.

With: Robert Taylor (Ivanhoe), Elizabeth Taylor (Rebecca), Joan Fontaine (Rowena), George Sanders (De Bois-Guilbert), Emlyn Williams (Wamba), Robert Douglas (Sir Hugh De Bracy), Finlay Currie (Cedric), Felix Aylmer (Isaac)

Saxon knight Ivanhoe (Robert Taylor) attempts to restore King Richard the Lionheart to the throne stolen from him by his brother, Prince John. Elizabeth Taylor plays Rebecca, who sacrifices her love for Ivanhoe in favour of Rowena (Joan Fontaine) to whom he is betrothed.

THE GIRL WHO HAD EVERYTHING (US 1952)

Prod/Armand Deutsch. Dir/Richard Thorpe. Scr/Art Cohn, based on the novel by Adela Rogers St Johns. Ph/Paul Vogel. Music/Andre Previn. GB distribution/Metro-Goldwyn-Mayer. Certificate A. 70 mins.

With: Elizabeth Taylor (Jean Latimer), Fernando Lamas (Victor Y Ramondi), William Powell (Seve Latimer), Gig Young (Vance Court), James Whitmore (Charles 'Chico' Menlow)

Jean (Taylor) is the daughter of wealthy criminal lawyer Steve Latimer, who is horrified to learn that she wishes to marry gang boss Victor Ramondi (Fernando Lamas), whom he has been defending in a court case. If Vic insists on marrying Jean, Steve threatens to appear before a criminal investigation committee with testimony convicting him of a long list of offences.

RHAPSODY (US 1952)

Prod/Lawrence Weingarten. Dir/Charles Vidor. Scr/Fay and Michael Kanin, based on the novel 'Maurice Guest' by Henry Handel Richardson. Ph/Robert Planck. Technicolor. Music director/John Green. Piano recordings/Claudio Arran. Violin recordings/Michael Rabin GB distribution/Metro-Goldwyn-Mayer. Certificate U. 116 mins.

With: Elizabeth Taylor (Louise Durant), Vittorio Gassman (Paul Bronte), John Ericson (James Guest)

When Louise Durant (Taylor) is jilted by her fiancé Paul Bronte (Vittorio Gassman), aspiring concert pianist James Guest (John Ericson) sacrifices his musical ambitions to marry her. When he discovers that she still cares for Paul, he turns to drink and gradually begins to destroy himself. Realising what is happening to her husband, Louise persuades him to return to his music. He agrees, but after weeks of study and

Opposite: in Raintree County

devotion, it is only at James's successful concert début, that Louise realises she is at last free of her attachment to Paul.

ELEPHANT WALK (US 1954)

Prod/Irving Asher. Dir/William Dieterle. Scr/John Lee Mahin, based on the novel by Robert Standish. Ph/Loyal Griggs. Technicolor. Music/Franz Waxman. GB distribution/ Paramount. Certificate U. 103 mins.

With: Elizabeth Taylor (Ruth Wiley), Dana Andrews (Dick Carver), Peter Finch (John Wiley), Abraham Sofaer (Appuhamy), Abner Biberman (Dr Pereira)

Loaned to Paramount to replace Viven Leigh, whom she was required to match exactly (since the studio did not want to waste the footage they had already shot), Taylor did not enjoy making *Elephant Walk*. Cast as Ruth Larkin, the English wife of Ceylon tea plantation owner John Wiley (Peter Finch), she has to cope with her husband's obsessive devotion to the memory of his dead father, and the open advances of her husband's assistant Dick Carver (Dana Andrews). Surviving these emotional traumas and a cholera epidemic, she is finally rendered helpless when an elephant herd stampede the range to claim back their ancient trail.

This page: in The Only Game in Town

Opposite: in Raintree County

BEAU BRUMMELL (GB 1954)

Prod/Sam Zimbalist. Dir/Curtis Bernhardt. Scr/Karl Tunberg, based on the play by Clyde Finch. Ph/Oswald Morris. Eastman colour. Music/Richard Addinsell. Costumes/Elizabeth Haffenden. GB distribution / Metro-Goldwyn-Mayer. Certificate U. 111 mins

With: Stewart Granger (Beau Brummell), Elizabeth Taylor (Lady Patricia), Peter Ustinov (Prince of Wales), Robert Morley (George III)

Stewart Granger played the Regency dandy who is left alone and penniless when his close relationship with the Prince of Wales (Peter Ustinov) comes to an end. Elizabeth Taylor, as Lady Patricia, supplied the romantic interest in this lavish remake of the 1924 version, which had starred John Barrymore.

THE LAST TIME I SAW PARIS (US 1954)

Prod/Jack Cummings. Dir/Robert Brooks. Scr/Julius J and Philip G Epstein, Richard Brooks, based on the story by F Scott Fitzgerald. Ph/Joseph Ruttenberg. Technicolor. Music/Conrad Salinger. GB distribution/Metro-Goldwyn-Mayer. Certificate A. 116 mins.

With: Elizabeth Taylor (Helen Ellswirth), Van Johnson (Charles Wills), Walter Pidgeon (James Ellswirth), Donna Reed (Marion Ellswirth), Eva Gabor (Lorraine Quarl), Roger Moore (Paul)

This up-dated version of F Scott Fitzgerald's story starred Van Johnson as Charles Willis, a writer who returns to Paris to obtain custody of his daughter, living with his sister-in-law, Marion (Donna Reed). Sitting in a café, he recalls his past romances in Paris during World War II, and his failed marriage to Helen (Taylor), now deceased.

GIANT (US 1956)

Prod/George Stevens, Henry Ginsberg. Dir/George Stevens. Scr/Fred Guiol, Ivan Moffatt, based on the novel of Edna Herber. Ph/William C Mellor. Warner colour. Music/Dimitri Tiomkin. Songs/"There's Never Been Anyone Else But You" and "Giant" by Paul Francis Webster and Dimitri Tiomkin. GB distribution/Warner Brothers. Certificate A. 197 mins.

With: Elizabeth Taylor (Leslie Benedict), Rock Hudson (Bick Benedict), James Dean (Jett Rink), Jane Withers (Vashti Snythe), Chill Wills (Uncle Bawley), Mercedes McCambridge (Luz Benedict), Carroll Baker (Luz Benedict

Opposite: in
Butterfield 8

II), Dennis Hopper (Jordan Benedict III)

This epic about family conflicts between cattle rancher Bick Benedict (Rock Hudson), his wife Leslie (Taylor) and their two children Jordy (Dennis Hopper) and Luz (Carroll Baker), spanned two generations and was a testing film for all concerned. James Dean gave his last performance and earned himself an Oscar nomination (as did Rock Hudson) for his portrayal of Jett Rink, the quarrelsome young ranch-hand who discovers oil on a small plot of inherited land and becomes enormously rich but eventually lonely and unloved. Towards the end of filming Taylor became ill and, when co-star Dean died in a car crash, she became so hysterical that director George Stevens had to shoot around her for two days.

RAINTREE COUNTRY (US 1957)

Prod/David Lewis. Dir/Edward Dmytryk. Scr/Millard Kaufman, based on the novel by Russ Lockridge Jr. Ph/ Robert Surtees. Technicolor. Music/Johnny Green. GB distribution/Metro-Goldwyn-Mayer. Certificate A. 166 mins.

With: Montgomery Clift (John Wickliff Shawnessy), Elizabeth Taylor (Susanna Drake), Eva Marie Saint (Nell

This page: with Warren Beatty in The Only Game in Town

Opposite: with Richard Burton in Cleopatra

Gaither), Nigel Patrick (Jerusalem Webster Stiles), Lee Marvin (Orville Flash Perkins), Rod Taylor (Garwood B Jones), Agnes Moorehead (Ellen Shawnessy)
Set during the American Civil War, the film tells the story of an ambitious Southern belle who woos and wins the man she thinks she wants, but subsequently finds life as a schoolmaster's wife boring. Co-starring with Taylor in this romantic melodrama was her old friend Montgomery Clift. Some critics described his performance as erratic, but the actor had changed considerably following a disastrous car accident after an evening with Elizabeth and her husband Michael Wilding. Nevertheless the film won Taylor an Oscar nomination and became a big commercial success.

CAT ON A HOT TIN ROOF (US 1958)

Prod/Lawrence Weingarten. Dir/Richard Brooks. Scr/Richard Brooks, James Pie, based on the play by Tennessee Williams. Ph/William Daniels. Metro colour. GB distribution/Metro-Goldwyn-Mayer. Certificate X. 108 mins.
With: Elizabeth Taylor (Maggie), Paul Newman (Brick), Burl Ives (Big Daddy), Jack Carson (Gooper), Judith Anderson (Big Mama)

This page: in The Only Game in Town

Opposite: in The VIPs

This Tennessee Williams-based story of mendacity uprooting a patriarchal Southern family had Burl Ives as Big Daddy Pollitt who, dying of cancer, finds little sympathy among his bickering family members. His son **Gooper** (Jack Carson) awaits Big Daddy's death so that he and his wife can inherit his huge fortune, while Brick (Paul Newman) the other son, is disinterested in the family fortune, preferring to drink heavily and brood about his younger days as a football hero. Alienated from his father by a desire for the outward show of love Big Daddy refuses, Brick will not sleep with his wife Maggie (Taylor) whom he continually rejects. Another reason for this is his latent homosexuality — an element revealed in the original play, but expurgated from the film's script because of Hollywood's moral code. Both Taylor and Newman received Oscar nominations for their fine acting.

SUDDENLY LAST SUMMER (GB 1959)
Prod/Sam Spiegel. Dir/Joseph L Mankiewicz. Scr/Gore Vidal, Tenessee Williams, adapted from the Tennessee Williams play. Ph/Jack Hildyard. Music/Baxton Orr, Malcolm Arnold. GB distribution/Columbia. Certificate X. 114 mins.
With: Elizabeth Taylor (Catherine Holly), Katherine Hepburn (Mrs Venables), Montgomery Clift (Dr Cukrowicz), Albert Dekker (Dr Hockstader), Mercedes McCambridge (Mrs Holly)
This dark Gothic tale, adapted from another Tennessee Williams' play, was about a young girl (Taylor) mentally disturbed after seeing her homosexual cousin killed by a horde of urchins. Her aunt (Katharine Hepburn) institutionalises her and arranges for a brain surgeon (Montgomery Clift) to have her lobotomised to prevent her from ever recounting the macabre scene and thus defiling the memory of her beloved son. Taylor was again nominated for an Oscar, along with Katharine Hepburn. "If there were ever any doubts about the ability of Miss Taylor to express complex and devious emotions, to deliver a flexible and deep performance, this film ought to remove them," stated the critic of the New York Herald Tribune.

BUTTERFIELD 8 (US 1960)
Prod/Pandro S Berman. Dir/Daniel Mann. Scr/Charles Schnee, John Michael Hayes, based on the novel by John O'Hara. Ph/Joseph Ruttenberg, Charles Harten. Cinema

Opposite: in The Taming of the Shrew

Scope, Metro colour. Music/Bronislau Kaper. GB distribution/ Metro-Goldwyn-Mayer. Certificate X. 108 mins.

With: Elizabeth Taylor (Gloria Wandrous), Laurence Harvey (Weston Liggett), Eddie Fisher (Steve Carpenter), Dina Merrill (Emily Liggett)

A high class prostitute named Gloria (Taylor) falls in love with a married man (Laurence Harvey) and is convinced she has found Mr Right. Their tempestuous relationship comes to a tragic end when Gloria succumbs to the thought that the love she wants so much can never be realised. However much Taylor hated the film, it won her the Oscar that she'd been chasing all her career. But, she later commented, "I knew my performance hadn't deserved it, that it was a sympathy award."

CLEOPATRA (US 1963)

Prod/Walter Wanger. Dir/Joseph L Mankiewicz. Second Unit directors/Ray Kellogg, Andrew Marton. Scr/Joseph L Mankiewicz, Ranald MacDougall, Sidney Buchman, based on Plutarch, Seutonius, Appian and C M Franzero's "The Life and Times of Cleopatra". Ph/Leon Shamroy. Second Unit ph/Claude Renoir, Piero Portalupi. Todd AO, DeLuxe

This page: with Michael Caine in Zee & Co

Opposite: in The Taming of the Shrew

colour. Music/Alex North. Costumes/Irene Sharaff
Choreography/Hermes Pan. GB distribution/20th Century
Fox. Certificate A. 226 mins. (Original running time
242 mins).

With: Elizabeth Taylor (Cleopatra), Richard Burton (Mark
Antony), Rex Harrison (**Julius Caesar**), Roddy MacDowall
(Octavian), Cesare Danova (Apollodorus), Hume Cronyn
(Sosigenes), Robert Stephens (Gemanicus), Kenneth Haigh
(Brutus), George Cole (Flavius), Martin Landau (Rufio),
Andrew Keir (Agrippa), Pamela Brown (High Priestess),
Isabelle Cooley (Charmain), Gwen Watford (Calpurnia),
Francesca Annis (Eiras)

One of the most costly films ever made, this Hollywood
extravaganza covers the rise and fall of the Roman Empire
starting with Cleopatra (Taylor) meeting Julius Caesar (Rex
Harrison) when he arrives as conqueror of Egypt, and ending
with her suicide, and that of her lover's, Mark Antony
(Richard Burton) following the defeat of Rome. Having
already suffred $7 million worth of setbacks and the
near-death of its star, the trouble-plagued production
switched location from London to Rome taking with it a new
director, cinematographer, costume designer and sixty new
sets. In addition, Peter Finch and Stephen Boyd (the original
Caesar and Mark Antony) were replaced. Visually splendid
but inordinately long, no film had ever been as heavily
pre-sold or widely publicised as this $30 million production.
During filming, the love affair between Taylor and Burton
became a real-life romance of legendary proportions.

THE VIPS (GB 1963)

Prod/Anatole de Grunwald. Dir/Anthony Asquith. Scr/
Terence Rattigan. Ph/Jack Hildyard. Panavision, Metro
colour. Music/Miklos Rozsa. Costumes/Givenchy. GB
distribution / Metro-Goldwyn-Mayer. Certificate A.
119 mins.

With: Elizabeth Taylor (Frances Andros), Richard Burton
(Paul Andros), Louis Jourdan (Marc Champselle), Elsa
Martinelli (Gloria Gritti), Margaret Rutherford (Duchess of
Brighton), Maggie Smith (Miss Mead), Rod Taylor (Les
Mangrum), Orson Welles (Max Buda), Linda Christian
(Miriam Marshall), Dennis Price (Commander Millbank),
Richard Wattis (Sanders), Ronald Fraser (Joslin), David
Frost (Reporter)

Opposite: in Zee
& Co
Shrewdley cashing in on the much publicised liason between

Taylor and Burton, MGM hired them to star in this glossy story about a group of wealthy passengers having to spend the night in a hotel when their airplane is grounded by fog. Burton plays millionaire shipping magnate Paul Andros, trying to prevent his wife Frances (Taylor) from leaving him and having an affair with French playboy Marc Champselle (Louis Jourdan). Most of the acting honours went to Margaret Rutherford as the eccentric Duchess of Brighton, while Maggie Smith gave a memorable performance as Miss Mead, the faithful secretary secretly in love with her boss, Les Mangrum (Rod Taylor).

THE SANDPIPER (US 1965)

Prod/Martin Ransohoff. Dir/Vincente Minnelli. Scr/Dalton Trumbo, Michael Wilson, based on the story by Martin Ransohoff. Ph/Milton Krasner. Wildlife photography/Richard Borden. Panavision. Metro colour. Music/Johnny Mandell. Lyrics/Paul Francis Webster. Costumes/Irene Sharaff. Laura's paintings/Elizabeth Duquette. Redwood sculpture/Edmund Kara. GB distribution/Metro-Goldwyn-Mayer. Certificate A. 117 mins.
With: Elizabeth Taylor (Laura Reynolds), Richard Burton (Edward Hewitt), Eva Marie Saint (Clare Hewitt), Charles

This page: with Peter O'Toole in Under Milkwood

Opposite: in Zee & Co

Bronson (Cos), Robert Webber (Ward Hendricks), Morgan Mason (Danny Reynolds)

Artist Laura Reynolds (Taylor) and her nine-year-old son live alone in a Monterey beach shack. When she is forced to enrol him at a local school, she attracts the attention of the headmaster, a married priest named Edward Hewitt (Richard Burton). The couple fall in love but, unlike the carefree Laura, Hewitt is guilt-ridden about having betrayed his wife Clare (Eva Marie Saint). Forgetting his personal agony, he decides that he must uphold his moral integrity and responsibility to the ideals of education. Finally recognised as a painter of rare talent, Laura is allowed to withdraw her son from school and continue, as she had done in the past, to teach him about life by herself.

WHO'S AFRAID OF VIRGINIA WOOLF? (US 1966)

Prod/Ernest Lehman. Dir/Mike Nichols. Scr/Ernest Lehman, based on the play by Edward Albee. Ph/Haskell Wexler. Music / Alex North. Costumes / Irene Sharaff. GB distribution/Warner-Pathe. Certificate X. 132 mins.

With: Elizabeth Taylor (Martha), Richard Burton (George), George Segal (Nick), Sandy Dennis (Honey)

George (Burton), a waspish university professor, is the henpecked husband of Martha (Taylor), whose loud-mouthed vulgarity covers up tumultuous frustrations and a deep feminine vulnerability. Late one Saturday night they come home from a party and await the arrival of Nick (George Segal), a new tutor at George's college, and his wife Honey (Sandy Dennis). The young couple are subsequently drawn into an all-night shouting match that peels away the corrosive layers of George and Martha's self-destructive, embittered marriage. It is a night from which none of the four people emerge unscathed. Mike Nichols' film won Taylor her second Oscar. Traditionally seen as a screen beauty, it was the first time she appeared as a battered old hag — greying and overweight. Violating nearly every section of Hollywood's code of conduct, the realistic and (at the time) shockingly explicit language broke new ground in film dialogue. "One of the most scathingly honest American films ever made," commented critic Stanley Kauffmann.

THE TAMING OF THE SHREW (US/Italy 1966)

Prod/Richard Burton, Elizabeth Taylor, Franco Zeffirelli. Dir/Franco Zeffirelli. Scr/the play by Shakespeare, adapted

Opposite: in Zee & Co

by Paul Dehn, Suso Cecchi D'Amico, Franco Zeffirelli. Ph/ Oswald Morris, Lusiano Trasatti. Panavision, Technicolour. Music/Nino Rota. Costumes/Irene Sharaff, Danilo Donati. GB distribution/BLC-Columbia. Certificate U. 122 mins. (English dialogue).

With: Richard Burton (Petruchio), Elizabeth Taylor (Katharina), Michael Hordern (Baptista), Cyril Cusack (Grumio), Michael York (Lucentio), Alfred Lynch (Tranio), Natasha Pyne (Bianca), Alan Webb (Gremio), Victor Spinetti (Hortensio)

Taylor was well cast as the fiery Katharina for whom a husband must be found before her younger sister Bianca (Natasha Pyne) can marry, in Franco Zeffirelli's adaptation of Shakespeare's play. The story tells how a wily and robust suitor named Petruchio (Burton) woos and then tames the tempestuous Katharina, when all others have failed. It was chosen for the Royal Film Performance of 1966.

This page: with Richard Burton in Hammersmith is Out

Opposite: in Hammersmith is Out

DOCTOR FAUSTUS (GB/Italy 1967)

Prod/Richard Burton, Richard McWhorter. Dir/Richard Burton, Nevill Coghill. Scr/Nevill Coghill, adapted from the play "The Tragic History of Doctor Faustus" by Christopher

Marlowe, Ph/Gabor Pogany. Technicolor. Music/Mario Nascimbene. GB distribution/Columbia. Certificate X. 93 mins.

With: Richard Burton (Doctor Faustus), Andreas Teuber (Mephistopheles), Elizabeth Taylor (Helen of Troy), Ian Marter (Emperor), Elizabeth O'Donovan (Empress), David McIntosh (Lucifer), Jeremy Eccles (Belzebub)

The story concerns a medieval doctor's attempt to master all human knowledge by selling his soul to the Devil. Taylor had a cameo part as Helen of Troy, who promises Burton, in the title role, a fate worse than death as she beckons him down an escalator into the fires of hell at the end of the film.

REFLECTIONS IN A GOLDEN EYE (US 1967)

Prod/Ray Stark. Dir/John Huston. Scr/Chapman Mortimer, Gladys Hill, based on the novel by Carson McCullers. Ph/ Aldo Tonti. Panavision. Technicolor. Music/Toshiro Mayuzumi. GB distribution/Warner-Pathe. Certificate X. 109 mins.

With: Marlon Brando (Major Weldon Penderton), Elizabeth Taylor (Leonora Penderton), Brian Keith (Lt Col Morris Langdon), Julie Harris (Alison Langdon), Zorro David (Annacleto)

Taylor played a frustrated, teasing wife in John Huston's film about an army Major (Brando) who comes tortuously to realise that he is a latent homosexual. Tragedy arises when he misconstrues the attentions of a young Private (Robert Forster) who is in fact obsessed with the Major's wife. The part of the Major was originally intended for Montgomery Clift but, after the actor's death in 1966, Brando took the role.

THE COMEDIANS (US/Bermuda/France 1967)

Prod-dir/Peter Glenville, Scr/Graham Greene, based on his novel. Ph/Henri Decae. Panavision. Metro colour. Music/ Laurence Rosenthal. GB distribution/Metro-Goldwyn-Mayer. Certificate X. 147 mins. (Original running time 156 mins).

With: Richard Burton (Brown), Alec Guinness (Major Jones), Elizabeth Taylor (Martha Pineda), Peter Ustinov (Ambassador Pineda), Paul Ford (Mr Smith), Lillian Gish (Mrs Smith), George Stanford Brown (Henri Philpot), Roscoe Lee Brown (Petit Pierre), Gloria Foster (Madame Philpot), James Earl Jones (Dr Magiot), Zacks Mokae (Michel), Raymond St Jacques (Capt Concasseur), Douta Seck (Joseph), Cicely Tyson (Marie Therese)

Opposite: in Night Watch

Overleaf: in Night Watch

Haiti, fermenting with ruthless dictatorship and political intrigues on the part of the secret police, is the setting for this drama in which a group of people find themelves drawn into the vortex of the island's revolution-torn régime. Richard Burton plays Brown, a hotel owner who has a passionate affair with Martha Pineda (Taylor), wife of a South American ambassador portrayed by Peter Ustinov. It was said that Taylor took half her normal salary for this picture, after it was suggested that her part be offered to Sophia Loren.

BOOM! (GB 1968)

Prod/John Heyman, Norma Priggen. Dir/Joseph Losey. Scr/ Tennessee Williams, based on his play "The Milk Train Doesn't Stop Here Anymore" adapted from his story, "Man, Bring This Up Road". Ph/Douglas Slocombe. Panavision. Technicolor. Music/John Barry. Indian music/Nazirali Jairazbnoy, Viram Jasani. Song "Hideaway" by John Dankworth, Don Black, sung by Georgie Fame. Costumes/ Tiziani. GB distribution/Rank. Certificate X. 113 mins.
With: Elizabeth Taylor (Flora Goforth), Richard Burton (Chris Flanders), Noel Coward (Witch of Capri), Joanne Shimkus (Blackie), Michael Dunn (Rudy), Romolo Valli (Dr Lullo), Veronica Wells (Simonetta), Fernando Piazza (Giulio), Howard Taylor (Journalist)
Flora Goforth, a widowed semi-recluse of enormous wealth and power who rules despotically over her own private volcanic island, embarks upon her last romance with a wandering poet named Chris Flanders (Richard Burton). Directed by Joseph Losey and based on Tennessee William's "The Milk Train Doesn't Stop Here Anymore," *Boom!* marked the Burtons' eighth film together.

SECRET CEREMONY (GB 1968)

Prod/John Heyman, Norman Priggen. Dir/Joseph Losey. Scr/ George Tabori, based on a story by Marco Denevi. Ph/ Gerry Fisher. Eastman colour. Music/Richard Rodney Bennett. Costumes/Dior. GB distribution/Rank. Certificate X. 109 mins.
With: Elizabeth Taylor (Leonora), Mia Farrow (Cenci), Robert Mitchum (Albert), Pamela Brown (Aunt Hilda), Peggy Ashcroft (Aunt Hanna)
Another Losey-directed picture, the strange story told of the relationship between a fading prostitute (Taylor) and a young girl who insists that she is her mother. Fascinated by this waif-

Previous page: in Ash Wednesday

Opposite: in Ash Wednesday

life creature who resembles her dead young daughter, Taylor takes her in and gradually becomes devoted to her, even though they come to realise that they are not after all related.

THE ONLY GAME IN TOWN (US 1969)

Prod/Fred Kohlmar. Dir/George Stevens. Scr/Frank D Gilroy, based on his play. Ph/Henri Decae. DeLuxe colour. Music/Maurice Jarre. Costumes/Mia Fonssagraves, Vicki Tiel. GB distribution/20th Century-Fox. Certificate A. 113 mins.

With: Elizabeth Taylor (Fran Walker), Warren Beatty (Joe Grady), Charles Braswell (Thomas Lockwood), Hank Henry (Tony), Olga Valery (Woman in purple wig)

For several years chorus girl Fran Walker (Taylor) has waited for her erstwhile lover Thomas Lockwood (Charles Braswell) to get divorced so that they can marry. One bored night she walks downtown into a second-rate bar where she meets piano player Joe Grady (Warren Beatty). The two fall in love, but their relationship is strained by his compulsive gambling. After an evening in which Joe loses everything, he decides to give up gambling for good and embark upon a new life with Fran.

This page: with Laurence Harvey in Night Watch

Opposite: in Ash Wednesday

ZEE & CO (US: X, Y & ZEE) (GB 1971)

Prod/Jay Kanter, Alan Ladd Jr. Dir/Brian G Hutton. Scr/
Edna O'Brien. Ph/Billy Williams. Music/Stanley Myers.
Songs "Going in Circles" by Ted Meyers, Jaiananda;
"Whirlwind" by Rick Wakeman, Dave Lambert; "Gladys'
Party" by John Mayer. Costumes/Beatrice Dawson. GB
distribution/Columbia-Warner. Certificate X. 109 mins.
With: Elizabeth Taylor (Zee Blakeley), Michael Caine
(Robert Blakeley), Susannah York (Stella), Margaret
Leighton (Gladys), John Standing (Gordon)
Robert Blakeley (Michael Caine) and his wife Zee (Taylor)
share a stormy married life that revolves around Zee's volatile
temperament. When Robert meets Stella (Susannah York) at
a party, he is immediately attracted to her warm and friendly
personality. They strike up a relationship that is both calm
and loving — in deep contrast to Robert's marriage. When
Robert finally tells Zee that he plans to leave her for Stella,
his wife is determined to keep her husband by fair means or
foul.

UNDER MILK WOOD (GB 1971)

Exec. Prod/Hugh French, Jules Buck. Dir-scr/Andrew
Sinclair, based on the radio play by Dylan Thomas. Ph/Bob
Huke. Technicolor. Music/Brian Gascoigne. GB distribution/
Rank. Certificate AA. 88 mins.
With: Richard Burton (First Voice), Elizabeth Taylor (Rosie
Probert), Peter O'Toole (Captain Cat), Glynis Johns
(Myfanwy Price), Vivien Merchant (Mrs Pugh), Sian Phillips
(Mrs Ogmore-Pritchard), Victor Spinetti (Mog Edwards),
Ryan Davies (Second Voice), Angharad Rees (Gossamer
Beynon)
Taylor played a small role as Rosie Probert in this look at life
in the Welsh village of Llaneggub, as seen through the eyes of
poet Dylan Thomas.

HAMMERSMITH IS OUT (US 1972)

Prod/Alex Lucas. Dir/Peter Ustinov. Scr/Stanford
Whitmore. Ph/Richard H Kline. Du Art colour. Music/
Dominic Frontiere. GB distribution/Cinerama. Certificate
X. 114 mins.
With: Elizabeth Taylor (Jimmie Jean Jackson), Richard
Burton (Hammersmith), Peter Ustinov (Doctor), Beau
Bridges (Billy Breedlove), George Raft (Guido Scartucci)
This black farce revolves around Hammersmith (Richard

*Opposite: in
Ash
Wednesday*

Burton), a homicidal inmate of a mental asylum. Billy Breedlove (Beau Bridges) is a dumb male nurse who helps Hammersmith escape when the inmate promises to give him the world. Billy soon becomes a puppet manipulated by Hammersmith, who uses him to become one of the most influential men in the country. Taylor plays Jimmie Jean Jackson, Billy's girlfriend and one of life's losers.

NIGHTWATCH (GB 1973)
Prod/Martin Poll, George W George, Bernard Straus. Dir/ Brian G Hutton. Scr/Tony Williamson, based on the play by Lucille Fletcher. Ph/Billy Williams. Technicolor. Music/ John Cameron. Costumes/Valentino. GB distribution/Avco-Embassy. Certificate X. 98 mins.
With: Elizabeth Taylor (Ellen Wheeler), Laurence Harvey (John Wheller), Billie Whitelaw (Sarah Cooke), Robert Lang (Appleby), Tony Britton (Tony), Bill Bean (Inspector Walker), Linda Hayden (Girl in car)
This was a tale about a housewife named Ellen (Taylor) who claims to have seen the body of a murder victim in the house at the bottom of her garden. Solicitous of her state of mind, her husband John (Laurence Harvey) calls the police but their

This page: with Robert Lang in Night Watch

Opposite: a 1975 publicity shot

investigations prove fruitless. Doubts concerning Ellen's sanity are strengthened when she maintains that she has seen a second murder victim in the house. The film marked Harvey's last screen appearance, whose death in 1973 was much lamented by close friend Taylor.

ASH WEDNESDAY (US 1973)

Prod/Dominick Dunne. Dir/Larry Peerce. Scr/Jean-Claude Tramont. Ph/Ennio Guarnieri. Technicolor. Music/Maurice Jarre. Costumes/Edith Head. GB distribution/Scotia-Barber. Certificate AA. 99 mins.

With: Elizabeth Taylor (Barbara Sawyer), Henry Fonda (Mark Sawyer), Helmut Berger (Erich), Keith Baxter (David), Maurice Teynac (Dr Lambert), Margaret Blye (Kate)

While staying in Italy, Barbara Sawyer (Taylor), a middle-aged, gone-to-seed woman in her fifties, undergoes head-to-toe cosmetic surgery in a desperate attempt to win back the love of her husband Mark (Henry Fonda). Having recaptured her former good looks, Barbara is pleased by the subsequent attraction of several young men, but remains faithful to her husband who is due to visit her. Only after a reunion with her daughter, who lets slip that Mark is due to ask his wife for a divorce, does Barbara succumb to the advances of Erich (Helmut Berger), with whom she has a fleeting affair. Eventually she is visited by Mark. Seeing her for the first time since the surgery, he feels both moved and guilt-ridden when he realises what she has been through in order to try and save their marriage. Sadly, he still maintains that they no longer satisfy each other's needs and the couple reach a decision about their future.

IDENTIKIT (Italy 1974)

Prod/Franco Rossellini. Dir/Giuseppe Patroni Griffi. Scr/Raffaele La Capria, Guiseppe Patroni Griffi, based on the novel by Muriel Spark. Music/Franco Mannio. GB distribution (Not set). 105 mins.

With: Elizabeth Taylor, Ian Bannen, Mona Washbourne, Guido Mannari

Based on Muriel Spark's novel "The Driver's Seat," this film starred Taylor as a woman searching for the man whom she discovers is trying to destroy her. The film was never released in Britain.

Opposite: in A Little Night Music

THAT'S ENTERTAINMENT (US 1974)

Prod-dir-scr/Jack Haley Jr. Metrocolor. 70mm Stereophonic Sound. Additional music/Henry Mancini. GB distribution/CIC. Certificate U. 138 mins.

Narrators: Fred Astair, Bing Crosby, Gene Kelly, Peter Lawford, Liza Minnelli, Donald O'Connor, Debbie Reynolds, Mickey Rooney, Frank Sinatra, James Stewart, Elizabeth Taylor

This was a montage of memorable scenes from over 100 MGM musicals, and treated modern audiences to a delightful trip down Memory Lane. Jack Haley Jnr managed to persuade a whole roster of former MGM contract artists, including Taylor, to introduce various film clips. As Variety noted, "While many ponder the future of MGM, none can deny that it has one hell of a past."

THE BLUEBIRD (US/USSR 1975)

Prod/Edward Lewis. Director/George Cukor. Script/Alexei Kapler, Alfred Hayes, Colin Higgins, based on a metaphysical idyll by Maurice Maeterlinck. Ph/Music/Andrei Petrov, Alex North with the Kirov Opera Ballet and the Leningrad Symphony Orchestra. GB

This page: in A Little Night Music

Opposite: in The Mirror Crack'd

distribution/20th Century-Fox
With a multi-national cast and crew, this lavish fantasy (a remake of the 1950 version starring Shirley Temple) tells of two children seeking the blue bird of happiness and who, after many adventures, eventually discover it in their own back yard. The first co-production between America and Russia, *The Blue Bird* failed to live up to the talents of its star-studded cast. "It works so hard at making history," wrote one critic, 'that it forgets to make sense."

VICTORY IN ENTEBBE (US 1976)
Prod/Robert Guenette. Dir/Martin J Chomsky. Scr/Ernest Kinoy. Ph/James Kilgore. Music/Charles Fox. GB distribution/Columbia-Warner. Certificate A. 119 mins.
With: Helmut Berger (German hijacker), Theodore Bikel (Yakov), Linda Blair (Chana Vilnofsky), Kirk Douglas (Hershel Vilnofsky), Richard Dreyfuss (Col Yonni Netanyahu), Stefan Gierasch (Mordecai Gur), David Groh (Benyamin Wise), Julius Harris (President Idi Amin), Helen Hayes (Mrs Wise), Anthony Hopkins (Yitzhak Rabin), Burt Lancaster (Shimon Peres), Christian Marquand (Captain Dukas), Elizabeth Taylor (Edra Vilnofsky), Jessica Walters (Nomi Haroun), Harris Yulin (Gen Dan Shomron)
Originally filmed on videotape, this TV-movie was later transferred to film for theatrical release outside America. Taylor made a guest appearance in the recreation of the lightning raid made by Israeli commandos to rescue Jewish hostages held captive by Arab terrorists in Uganda. Anthony Hopkins and Burt Lancaster were impressive as the Israeli political leaders in Tel Aviv responsible for planning the rescue.

A LITTLE NIGHT MUSIC (US 1977)
Prod/Elliott Kastner. Dir/Harold Prince. Scr/Hugh Wheeler, based on the stage production and the Ingmar Bergman film *Smiles of a Summer Night*. Ph/Arthur Ibbetson. Music/ Stephen Sondheim. Choreography/Patricia Birch.
With: Elizabeth Taylor (Desiree Armfeldt), Diana Rigg (Charlotte Mittelheim), Len Cariou (Frederick Egerman), Hermione Gingold (Mme Armfeldt), Lesley-Anne Down (Anne Egerman), Laurence Guittard (Carl-Magnus Mittelheim), Christopher Guard (Erich Egerman), Lesley Dunlop (Petra), Chloe Franks (Frederika), Heinz Marecek (Kurt)

Opposite: in
The Mirror
Crack'd

Set in a small Austrian town, a stuffy married lawyer named Frederick Egerman (Len Cariou) recommences a love affair with his old flame Desirée (Taylor), whose current lover — a married Count — challenges him to a game of Russian roulette. It was an unpopular film version of Stephen Soundheim's stylised, and highly successful Broadway stage musical, despite offering the novelty of hearing Elizabeth Taylor sing "Send in the Clowns."

THE MIRROR CRACK'D (US 1977)

Murder results when Holywood producer Tony Curtis sets up the shooting of a new film in an English village. Taylor and Kim Novak play faded movie actresses making comebacks as Mary Queen of Scots and Elizabeth I in the film-within-a-film, while Angela Lansbury gives a faithful portrayal of Agatha Christie's sleuth, aided by dapper nephew Edward Fox, as Chief Inspector Craddock. As Taylor's director-husband, Rock Hudson re-teamed with the leading lady he starred with twenty-four years previously in *Giant* — in which they also played husband and wife.

This page: in The Mirror Crack'd

Opposite: with Rock Hudson in The Mirror Crack'd